ideals
THANKSGIVING

Vol. 46, No. 7

Publisher, Patricia A. Pingry
Executive Editor, Cynthia Wyatt
Art Director, Patrick McRae
Production Manager, Jeff Wyatt
Editorial Assistant, Kathleen Gilbert
Copy Editors, Marian Hollyday
　　　　　　　　Rhonda Colburn

ISBN 0-8249-1077-X

IDEALS—Vol. 46, No. 7 November 1989 IDEALS (ISSN 0019-137X) is published eight times a year: February, March, May, June, August, September, November, December by IDEALS PUBLISHING CORPORATION, Nelson Place at Elm Hill Pike, Nashville, Tenn. 37214. Second class postage paid at Nashville, Tennessee, and additional mailing offices. Copyright © 1989 by IDEALS PUBLISHING CORPORATION. POSTMASTER: Send address changes to Ideals, Post Office Box 148000, Nashville, Tenn. 37214-8000. All rights reserved. Title IDEALS registered U.S. Patent Office.

SINGLE ISSUE—$4.95
ONE-YEAR SUBSCRIPTION—eight consecutive issues as published $17.95
TWO-YEAR SUBSCRIPTION—sixteen consecutive issues as published—$31.95
Outside U.S.A., add $6.00 per subscription year for postage and handling.

ACKNOWLEDGMENTS
THE FIRST THANKSGIVING from *THE GREAT PLANTATION* by Clifford Dowdey, Copyright © 1957 by Clifford Dowdey. Used by permission; THE APPROACH OF THANKSGIVING from *A LITTLE BOOK OF TRIBUNE VERSE* by Eugene Field, 1901; THANKSGIVING from *THE LIGHT OF FAITH* by Edgar A. Guest, Copyright 1926 by The Reilly & Lee Co. All rights reserved. Used by permission; A THANKSGIVING FABLE by Oliver Herford from *THANKSGIVING,* Robert Haven Schauffler, ed., Copyright 1907 by Dodd, Mead & Company; COME HOME and THE LATCH UPON THE GATE by Douglas Malloch from *COME ON HOME,* Copyright 1923 by George H. Doran Company. Used by permission. Our sincere thanks to the following whose addresses we were unable to locate: Adelaide Blanton for PUMPKINS IN THE CORNFIELD; Hazel J. Fristad for THANKSGIVING GLADNESS; Sudie Stuart Hager for LET WINTER COME; Margaret H. Hasbargen for PLYMOUTH; Gertrude Jesser for BREAD IN THE BAKING; Mr. George B. Cavis for A GOOD THANKSGIVING by his aunt, Annie Douglas Green Robinson.

The paper used in this publication meets the minimum requirements of American National Standard for Information Sciences—Permanence of Paper for Printed Library Materials, ANSI 9.48-1984

Typesetting by The Font Shop, Nashville, Tennessee

Color Separation by Rayson Films, Inc., Waukesha, Wisconsin

Printing by W.A. Krueger Company, Brookfield, Wisconsin

Front and back covers
AUTUMN ABUNDANCE
H. Abernathy/H. Armstrong Roberts, Inc.

Photo Opposite
Gerald Koser

20　READERS' REFLECTIONS

24　COLLECTOR'S CORNER

26　FIFTY YEARS AGO

30　COUNTRY CHRONICLE

32　REST-OF-THE-BIRD CASSEROLES

34　THROUGH MY WINDOW

40　CRAFTWORKS

46　A SLICE OF LIFE

52　CHILD'S PLAY

54　FROM MY GARDEN JOURNAL

62　BITS AND PIECES

70　LEGENDARY AMERICANS

72　TRAVELER'S DIARY

80　READERS' FORUM

A Day of the Indian Summer

Sarah Helen Whitman

A day of golden beauty! Through the night
The hoarfrost gathered o'er each leaf and spray,
Weaving its filmy network thin and bright
And shimmering like silver in the ray
Of the soft sunny morning; turf and tree
Prance in its delicate embroidery,
And every withered stump and mossy stone
With gems encrusted and with seed pearl sown,
While in the hedge the frosted berries glow,
The scarlet holly and the purple sloe;
And all is gorgeous, fairy-like, and frail
As the famed gardens of the Arabian tale.
How soft and still the autumnal landscape lies,
Calmly outspread beneath the smiling skies
As if the earth, in prodigal array
Of gems and broidered robes, kept holiday—
Her harvest yielded and her work all done,
Basking in beauty 'neath the autumn sun!

Photo Opposite
LAVENDER CHRYSANTHEMUMS
Gene Ahrens

Color

Grace Noll Crowell

Have you noticed, have you seen
That God loves green?
And that he loves clear yellow too,
And blue—blue!
The trees, the sky, the glint of the sun,
The million yellow flowers that run
Their windy way;
And God loves gray:
The mist, the rain, the clouds that fly
When storms go by.
And looking at the dawn, I think
That God loves pink.
But red—have you ever thought how he
Uses it so sparingly?
A red flower here, another there,
A red wing flashing on the air,
A cluster of berries on a limb—
Red must be jewel-like to him
And very precious—but if I
Were asked the color I liked best,
'Twould be the color of the sky
Some autumn evening in the west:
Not mauve, not pink, not gold, not flame—
It has no name!

Photo Opposite
FALLING LEAVES AT SUNSET
Gay Bumgarner

GIVING THANKS

Joy Beehler Ward

Let's work our toil, then jacket up and go
Down by the pond and hear the geese fly south
And smell the hush of smoky pyres of leaves
Fallen in the last onslaught of wind
And feel the next gust brush our hair for us.
Let's well-preserve our house in glass and steam,
Then roam to glean the fields and autumn wood
For fruit and grain and homeless pods and seeds—
Refugees to shelter near our hearth
And share the bonding light of our new fire.
We have collected, canned, and sown and reaped
And stacked and heaped all summer into fall.
The table stretches into the next room.
The cloth is spread, the sideboard holds the feast.
Chrysanthemums are massed in earthy hues.
Let's give thanks.

Photo Opposite
FERNS AND FALL FOLIAGE
Ray Atkeson

Thanksgiving

Gene H. Osborne

What art Thou saying, Lord, to me
By the red-fruited tree—
The yellow pumpkin on its frosted vine—
The purple grapes down by the old stone wall—
The tangle of late asters—silken cornstalks tall—
Beauty of naked branches and a saffron sky,
That squadron of wild geese that southward fly?
Even the humble carrot hath an orange coat,
The beet a crimson robe—an onion silver skin.
By the rich walnut tree,
I see the gray squirrel scampering, filling winter bin.
The dainty weed beside the road doth yield
A perfect seed, wrought with divinest care;
Sometimes the wonder seems too great to bear.
O Lord, Thy beauteous bounty doth ensnare my soul!
I bow with great thanksgiving!

Photo Overleaf
THE ABUNDANT HARVEST
Grant Heilman

In the Time of Autumn

Minnie Klemme

Now in the time of autumn
When the harvest days are past,
When the scarlet leaf grows crisper
And the golden hours can't last,

There comes a time for sleeping
That the earth may have its rest;
For God so rules the seasons
To do what each knows best.

The birds have ceased their singing,
The nestlings long are gone,
A haze falls on the hillsides,
The frost brings rime at dawn.

Soon winter will be coming;
And when the time is right,
God beds the weary traveler
With a coverlet of white.

And in that winter's sleeping,
What dreams live 'neath the snow?
One day, one day in April,
The grass will let us know.

Photo Opposite
WOODLAND CLEARING IN AUTUMN
Bob Clemenz Photography

Photo Overleaf
SUGARHOUSE
NEAR LAKE WILLOUGHBY, VERMONT
Dick Dietrich

In Passing

S.H. Dewhurst

Now, on this corner of the year,
The Autumn stands a moment still
And wonders how it traveled here
So fast, so much against its will. . . .
It turns to grasp the threads of day,
Hoping yet to linger on;
But finding Winter in the way,
It rounds the corner and is gone.

Photo Opposite
HEMLOCK BRIDGE
MAINE
Dick Dietrich

PLYMOUTH

Margaret H. Hasbargen

Let anthems swell across the bay
Where once their ships at anchor lay;
Let flags unfurl upon the shore,
The threshold of our country's door.

Let all hearts join in humble prayer;
Let hymns of praise ring everywhere
Beyond that hallowed Plymouth sod
Where Pilgrims pledged their lives to God.

Let white stars float across blue skies;
Let red stripes brighten eager eyes;
Let organs sing of hills and plains
Till hearts repeat the glad refrains.

Let bells repeat with every chime
This prayer at Thanksgiving time:
God, guide our thoughts, lest we forget
That we are only pilgrims yet.

Photo Opposite
REPLICA OF THE MAYFLOWER
PLYMOUTH, MASSACHUSETTS
Fred Sieb

The First Feast

Jane G. Austin

Some late arrivals among the Indians had that morning brought in several large baskets of the delicious oysters for which Wareham is still famous; and although it was an unfamiliar delicacy to her, Priscilla, remembering a tradition brought from Ostend to Leyden by some travelers, compounded these with biscuit-crumbs, spices, and wine, and was looking about for an iron pan wherein to bake them, when Elizabeth Tilley brought forward some great clam and scallop shells which John Howland had presented to her, just as now a young man might offer a unique Sévres tea set to the lady of his love.

"Wouldn't it do to fill these with thy oyster compote, and so set them in the ashes to roast?" inquired she. "Being many they can be laid at every man's place at table."

"Why, 'tis a noble idea, child," exclaimed Priscilla eagerly. "'Twill be a novelty and will set off the board famously. Say you not so, John?"

"Ay," returned Alden, who was busily opening the oysters at her side. "And more by token there is a magnificence in the idea that thou hast not thought on; for as at a great man's table the silver dishes each bear the crest of his arms, so we being Pilgrims and thus privileged to wear the scallop shell in our hats, do rather choose to display it upon our board."

"Ah, John, thou hast an excellent wit—in *some* things," replied Priscilla with a half sigh which set the young fellow wondering for an hour.

By noon the long tables were spread, and still the sweet warm air of the Indian Summer made the out-of-door feast not only possible but charming,

for the gauzy veil upon the distant forest and the marine horizon and the curves of Captain's Hill seemed to shut in this little scene from all the world of turmoil and danger and fatigue, while the thick yellow sunshine filtered through with just warmth enough for comfort, and the sighing southerly breeze brought wafts of perfume from the forest and bore away, as it wandered northward, the peals of laughter, the merry yet discreet songs, and the multitudinous hum of blithe voices, Saxon and savage, male and female, adult and childish, that filled the dreamy air.

The oysters in their scallop shells were a singular success, and so were the mighty venison pasties, and the savory stew compounded of all that flies the air and all that flies the hunter in Plymouth woods, no longer flying now but swimming in glorious broth cunningly seasoned by Priscilla's anxious hand, and thick bestead with dumplings of barley flour, light, toothsome, and satisfying. Beside these were roasts of various kinds, and thin cakes of bread or manchets, and bowls of salad set off with wreaths of autumn leaves laid around them, and great baskets of grapes, white and purple, and of the native plum, delicious when fully ripe in its three colors of black, white, and red. With these were plentiful flagons of ale, for already the housewives had laid down the first brewing of the native brand and had moreover learned of the Indians to concoct a beverage akin to what is now called root beer, well flavored with sassafras, of which the Pilgrims had been glad to find good store since it brought a great price in the English market.

Jane Goodwin Austin is a nineteenth-century writer from Massachusetts. This excerpt from The First Thanksgiving Day of New England *is an example of her historical fiction about the Plymouth colonists which grew out of her research into her own family's experiences as first settlers of New England. Her best known work is a series of books for children about Pilgrims.*

19

After Summer

This autumn hush is golden-cool:
Blue shadows lie in midday sun;
The children's shouts are trapped in school,
And insect symphonies are done.

No breeze attends the slow leaf's fall,
And silent birds know song is lost.
A golden stillness muffles all,
And earth, resigned, awaits the frost.

Ruth DeLong Peterson
New London, Iowa

Thanksgiving

We recall that we studied as children
About a brave little Pilgrim crew
That sailed upon the *Mayflower*
To find a land they knew
Would bring them peace and happy homes
With religious freedom in living;
Thence this great festival came to be—
The celebration of Thanksgiving.

Let us think once more of our forefathers
When they reached the American shore
In December of 1620
During perilous days of yore.
A long, dreary winter lay before them,
Marked with hunger, disease, and cold;
And there were few who survived to relate
Those gripping experiences of old.

In the spring they courageously planted seed,
Toiling hard to make it grow;
And they were blessed with abundance
Before the first fall of snow.
They were happy and prepared a feast,
Gave thanks and recognition
For all the blessings that came their way,
Which thenceforth became a tradition.

In modern times at the close of harvest—
On the last Thursday in November,
Americans anticipate
A sumptuous turkey dinner
With family members gathered 'round
To commemorate anew and give
Humble thanks for this great heritage—
America, our home where we live.

Mildred S. Grave
Fort Dodge, Iowa

20

Reflections

Thanksgiving Gladness

I'm thankful that the Pilgrims wanted liberty,
That faith and courage made them cross the storm-tossed sea,
And glad their dauntless spirit, passed from man to man,
Has made me proud to be a staunch American.

I'm glad that in that autumn-time three hundred years ago,
With crops all gathered from the coming winter's snow,
The Pilgrims made the day which lives to cheer and bless
Each year with this, the day of prayer and thankfulness.

Oh, those were days when men were fearless, strong, and brave;
When womenfolk all had to manage, work, and save;
And, when I think of what their hardships must have been,
I'm thankful that I'm living now instead of then.

Hazel J. Fristad
Riverside, California

Autumn's Auctioneer

"It's going, going, gone
For all antiques,"
Old Weather called today,
For dandelions, once so gold,
But since arrayed in gray,
Were briskly bidden for
By Wind, and promptly
Whisked away!

L. E. Gleeson
Columbus, Ohio

Editor's Note: Readers are invited to submit unpublished, original poetry, short anecdotes, and humorous reflections on life for possible publication in future *Ideals* issues. Please send copies only; manuscripts will not be returned. Writers receive $10 for each published submission. Send material to "Readers' Reflections," Ideals Publishing Corporation, P.O. Box 140300, Nashville, Tennessee 37214-0300.

Harvest Hymn

John Greenleaf Whittier

Once more the liberal year laughs out
  O'er richer stores than gems or gold;
Once more with harvest-song and shout
  Is Nature's bloodless triumph told.

Oh, favors every year made new!
  Oh, gifts with rain and sunshine sent!
The bounty overruns our due,
  The fullness shames our discontent.

We shut our eyes, the flowers bloom on;
  We murmur, but the corn ears fill;
We choose the shadow, but the sun
  That casts it shines behind us still.

Who murmurs at his lot today?
  Who scores his native fruit and bloom?
Or sighs for dainties far away,
  Beside the bounteous board of home?

Thank Heaven, instead, that Freedom's arm
  Can change a rocky soil to gold—
That brave and generous lives can warm
  A clime with northern ices cold.

And let these altars, wreathed with flowers
  And piled with fruits, awake again
Thanksgivings for the golden hours,
  The early and the latter rain!

Give Thanks

Kay McKay

Today I mulched the roses,
Stored the summer bulbs away,
Played around in leaves of autumn;
'Twas a lovely, golden day.

Halloween is now behind us,
Ghosts and goblins faded out.
We have something more important
For us all to think about.

In the year of our forefathers—
It was 1621
When they held that first Thanksgiving
Amid prayer and feast and fun.

It had been a long, cold winter,
Many hardships felt by all.
Nearby Indians invited
Came in answer to the call.

'Twas the Pilgrims' first Thanksgiving—
Four wild turkeys graced the board
As they bowed their heads and gave thanks
To the God whom they adored.

Since that time we've greatly prospered,
Mighty nation—mighty men.
Could it be because our fathers
Held a first Thanksgiving then?

COLLECTOR'S CORNER

Cybis Porcelains

A Perfect Yellow Rose

There is a sense of deep reverence for nature in fine porcelain sculptures, a desire to re-create every perceivable, beautiful detail. Porcelain art combines the best of fine painting and sculpture. Flowers and birds can be created with marvelous, life-size realism, and miniature human figures executed in exquisite detail can have an almost magical presence.

The heritage of porcelain art is an old one which originated in ancient China and traveled west in the treasure bags of such explorers as Marco Polo who, fascinated by its purity, gave porcelain its name, calling it *porcellano* after the smooth, shiny seashells found along the shores of the Mediterranean.

The process by which porcelain is made remained unknown to the West until the eighteenth century when Johann Bottger duplicated the Chinese process in his studio in Poland. The great Meissen company grew out of Bottger's work, to be followed by porcelain art studios in France, Germany, Denmark, and England.

The oldest existing art porcelain studio in America is Cybis. The studio's porcelains enhance countless private homes and can be found in the White House and the residences of the United States Ambassador to the United Nations. The entire Cybis "North American Indian" Series is displayed at Blair House in Washington, D.C., our nation's official guesthouse for visiting dignitaries. Cybis sculptures are part of the permanent collections in many of the world's leading museums, including the preserver of American art and tradition, the Smithsonian Institution in Washington.

The studio's existence is a result of the vicissitudes of World War II. In 1938 Boleslaw Cybis, who received his artistic training at the Academy of Fine Arts in Warsaw, Poland, and his wife, Marja, an accomplished artist in her own right, came to the United States to paint a series of murals commissioned by their government in the Hall of Honor at the New York World's Fair. With their return to their homeland hindered after the outbreak of World War II, the Cybises chose to stay in the United States where they enjoyed artistic freedom to a greater extent than they had known in Poland.

Fifty years ago, in 1939, they established a studio in Astoria, New York, to create porcelain art in the fashion of the great European studios and soon moved to Trenton, New Jersey, historically the ceramic center of the United States. The success of this fine art studio is history: Cybis celebrates its fiftieth anniversary of fine art production this year.

Not all of the secrets of art porcelain are revealed to the public, but we do know that porcelain itself is created by mixing different types of clay with water until a silky-smooth liquid the consistency of heavy cream is formed. This creamy liquid is poured repeatedly into a mold until a

Elaine, Lady of the Lake

The Swan

buildup of layers has created a delicate porcelain shell. Once removed from the mold, the finishing of this shell involves many stages of delicate painting and carving by hand. The intricate details which characterize Cybis's designs are hand-crafted by the Cybis company of artists. Flowers are individually created, petal by petal. Bows are "tied" from clay ribbons. The long slender fingers so characteristic of Cybis sculptures must be carefully formed. Even the tiny creases and fingernails are carved by hand with the most delicate of tools.

Throughout its fifty years of operation, Cybis porcelains have portrayed a variety of subjects: the world of animals and flowers, characters from fairy tales, elegant portraits in porcelain, Madonnas, children, North American Indians, Christmas ornaments, gift collections, and bridal selections. Glazes applied in delicate pastel shades and highlighted with 24 karat liquid gold have become a Cybis tradition. Limited edition pieces usually do not exceed runs of 500 to 1,000, and sometimes are limited to twenty or thirty, creating irreplaceable treasures for the collector.

Throughout this golden year celebration, special collector's editions are enhanced with a golden anniversary back stamp. Sculptures already released for this year-long anniversary celebration include the beautiful *Scheherazade*, an animated sculpture of the Persian beauty who enthralled the king with her endless stories. This particular piece is part of the "Portraits of Porcelain" collection.

The celebration of nature's beauty often inspires artists to join the cause of preserving the earth's treasures. Cybis has become involved in a number of projects geared to enhance the world from which it derives inspiration. A notable example is the studio's project to aid endangered marine life through the sale of representative porcelain figures. The first two sculptures in the series, *The Humpback Whale* and *Arion, the Dolphin Rider*, were created with the scientific advice of Jean-Michel Cousteau, son of Jacques Costeau, the famed marine explorer whose signature appears on each sculpture. A percentage of the proceeds from the sale of these pieces is donated to the cause of preserving endangered marine life.

As with any serious art form, collecting fine porcelain art requires an initial investment. Collectors know that this investment accrues residuals with the passage of time, residuals both financial and aesthetic, to the joy of the proud art owner.

Phil Allen

Ballerina
Photography by Cybis

Phil Allen is the Vice-President of Operations at Cybis in Trenton, New Jersey.

Turkey Days

Whole United States Confused Over Conflicting Thanksgivings

Thirty days hath September,
April, June, and November.
All the rest have thirty-one
Until we hear from Washington.

Brooding over whether to observe Thanksgiving on Nov. 23, Nov. 30, or not at all, an Oklahoma official thus resorted to rhyme last week. In Kokomo, Ind., a shopkeeper hung out this sign: "Do your shopping now. Who knows, tomorrow may be Christmas." Throughout the nation the institution of Thanksgiving, originally an expression of gratitude on the completion of harvests, had become the object of humorous remarks. It was all because President Roosevelt had decided that an earlier holiday would help Christmas shopping (NEWSWEEK, Aug. 28).

While the governors of 23 states lined up behind the President, proclaiming Nov. 23 as Thanksgiving, and 22 others just as firmly plumped for the traditional last Thursday in November, Gov. W. Lee O'Daniel of Texas solved the problem by proclaiming both days. Maine and Colorado followed for legal reasons.

Denver and most Colorado cities had planned to follow the President's lead anyway, although Gov. Ralph L. Carr, a Republican, proclaimed Nov. 30. Then Attorney General Byron Rogers, a Democrat, ruled that the Presidential and gubernatorial ukases had equal standing. With schools, stores, and official agencies looking forward to two holidays, Carr announced sorrowfully that he would eat no turkey on the 23rd.

Attorney General Franz V. Burkett of Maine pointed out that by law the state must observe all Presidential proclamations. But that did not reflect the attitude of the rest of New England, whose official indignation was keynoted by Gov. Leverett Saltonstall of Massachusetts when he declared that the day was set apart to give thanks to God, "and not for the inauguration of Christmas shopping."

Ocala, Fla., nearly celebrated on Nov. 13, until a typographical error in the mayor's proclamation was rectified. But first prize for independence went to McGregor, Texas, where the mayor and business leaders cried "Nuts and cranberries" to both official dates, announcing that the town would splurge on Friday, Nov. 24, when the McGregor High School football team tangles with the eleven from Gatesville.

Missouri will observe Nov. 23, doubtless under some pressure from Gov. Lloyd C. Stark, whose 55th birthday and eighth wedding anniversary fall on that day. Across the border in Kansas, the celebration will take place a week later. North and South Dakota will split, the northerners taking the 23rd and the southerners the 30th. North and South Carolina disagree too.

Gov. Julius P. Heil of Wisconsin was only partly successful in opposing the President. Even before Attorney General John E. Martin ruled both proc-

President Franklin Delano Roosevelt poses with carving utensils ready to carve the Thanksgiving turkey. His decision to change Thanksgiving Day to the third week in November was intended to benefit merchants with a longer Christmas shopping period.

lamations official, the mayors of Milwaukee and Madison chose the 23rd. And Badger State residents found ample precedent for almost any date. Since 1836 Wisconsin has celebrated Thanksgiving variously from Nov. 20 to Dec. 17, and once the governor picked a Wednesday.

California, Oregon, and Washington will officially observe the 23rd, but several towns plan to default in each. Clarkston, Wash., will celebrate on the last Thursday along with Lewiston, Idaho, its larger twin on the south bank of the Snake River. Stanford University, at Palo Alto, Calif., where ex-President Herbert Hoover makes his home, is ignoring the President's proclamation, "due to previous commitments."

Schools in general have been upset by the con-fusion over dates. In many cases students will get vacations, but their parents in other cities or states will be at work that day. Gov. Robert L. Cochran of Nebraska won't have the pleasure of putting turkey before his son, who is enrolled at Culver Military Academy in Indiana. Nebraska will celebrate on the 30th and Indiana on the 23rd.

. . . From Washington Mr. Roosevelt notified Plymouth, Mass., where Thanksgiving originated, that because of a "tentative engagement already made," he could not attend Nov. 30 ceremonies there.

NEWSWEEK, Nov. 20, 1939

Photo Overleaf
CHURCH IN AUTUMN
SUGARHILL, NEW HAMPSHIRE
Gene Ahrens

Country
CHRONICLE
—— Lansing Christman ——

As I was closing the vents under our home in the Carolina hills, I found myself meditating about what it would be like to return to the era before paved roads brought automobiles out into farm country. I remembered my young years in the Northeast when we banked the house with October's fallen leaves at Thanksgiving time. We carried leaves by the barrelfuls to spread and pack along the foundation, holding them in place with weathered boards on which we piled stones to make them firm. Nothing was wasted in the country. Even the fallen leaves were good insulation against the long cold days and nights ahead.

How restricted farm life was when I was a boy! We had no electricity, and none of the modern appliances and conveniences which are now so much a part of nearly every household. Our radio was a "whiskered" contraption called a crystal set. Yet, how good and wholesome farm life was in the fall. Plowing was done; the harvests were in. Trees

stood stark and lean against gray November skies. Winter was sure to follow quickly on the heels of the festive day, Thanksgiving.

Then we would be spending days in the wood-lot, working up next year's supply of firewood with ax and saw in company with chickadees and nuthatches, woodpeckers and jays who pecked at our woodchips which speckled the snowy ground. Winters would be long and hard, but we accepted them with grace as part of the never-ending cycle of life. Our labors against the cold warmed us with the sense of keeping stride with nature's phases, of belonging to the earth.

At day's end there was time for visiting, for reading and writing, for sitting by the fireside with books and newspapers, apples and popcorn. There was a close-knit companionship in the home. We were blessed with the beauty of the snow-covered countryside, and blessed with the true meaning of Thanksgiving, of God's providence, of home and love and genuine family unity.

The author of two published books, Lansing Christman has been contributing to Ideals *for almost twenty years. Mr. Christman has also been published in several American, foreign, and braille anthologies. He and his wife, Lucile, live in rural South Carolina where they enjoy the pleasures of the land around them.*

Rest-of-the-Bird Casseroles

Turkey-Broccoli Casserole

Serves 6

- 2 10-ounce packages frozen broccoli or 2 bunches fresh broccoli
- 4 cups of cubed cooked turkey
- 1 cup mayonnaise
- 2 10¾-ounce cans condensed cream of chicken soup
- 1 teaspoon curry powder
- 1 tablespoon lemon juice
- ½ cup grated Cheddar cheese
- ½ cup bread crumbs
- 1 tablespoon melted butter or margarine

Steam broccoli until tender; drain. Grease an 11×7-inch casserole. Place turkey on the bottom and arrange broccoli over turkey. Combine mayonnaise, soup, curry powder, and lemon juice. Pour over broccoli. Combine cheese, bread crumbs, and butter; sprinkle over casserole. Bake in a 350° oven for 30 minutes.

Layered Turkey Casserole

Serves 8

- 3 eggs, beaten
- 1 cup milk or ½ cup milk and ½ cup cream of celery soup
- ¼ teaspoon salt
- ½ teaspoon dry mustard
- ½ teaspoon Worcestershire sauce
- 5 slices slightly stale bread, crusts trimmed
- 1 cup grated sharp Cheddar cheese
- ½ pound sliced or cubed cooked turkey

Combine eggs, milk, salt, mustard, and Worcestershire sauce. Grease a 9×13-inch casserole. Alternate layers of bread, turkey, and cheese, ending with bread. Cover with the liquid mixture and refrigerate for 4 hours or overnight. Bring to room temperature and bake in a 350° oven for 45 to 60 minutes. Let stand 15 minutes before serving.

Turkey Tetrazzini

Serves 6

- ¼ cup + 2 tablespoons butter or margarine
- ¼ cup + 2 tablespoons flour
- 1½ teaspoons salt
-   Dash nutmeg
- 2 cups milk
- 1 cup turkey or chicken stock
- 2 egg yolks
- ¾ cup milk
- ½ pound spaghetti, uncooked
- ½ pound mushrooms, sliced
- ½ cup diced onion
- 2 tablespoons butter or margarine
- 3 cups cubed cooked turkey
- 1½ cups grated Swiss or Meunster cheese

Melt butter in a large saucepan. Remove from heat and stir in flour, salt, and nutmeg. Gradually add 2 cups milk and stock and bring to a boil, stirring constantly. Boil 2 minutes or until slightly thickened. In a small bowl beat egg yolks with remaining milk. Pour 2 tablespoons hot mixture into yolks and then pour yolk mixture into saucepan, beating constantly until sauce is hot. DO NOT BOIL. Remove from heat. Cook spaghetti as directed on package; drain and return to pan. Remove 1 cup sauce and toss lightly with spaghetti. Place spaghetti in a 9×13-inch baking dish, creating a well in the center. Sauté mushrooms and onion in remaining butter. Add mushrooms, onion, and turkey to 1 cup of sauce. Reserve remaining sauce. Spoon turkey mixture into well in spaghetti. Sprinkle with cheese and cover with foil. Refrigerate 1 hour or overnight. Leaving foil on, bake in a 350° oven for 45 minutes. Heat reserved sauce and serve with casserole.

Note: Casserole can be frozen. Let thaw 1 hour and bake, covered, in a 350° oven 60 minutes or until bubbly.

THROUGH MY WINDOW

Pamela Kennedy

"But there won't be any family!" I hadn't meant to come out with such a wail, but my tone betrayed my feelings. Thanksgiving was only three weeks away and we were stuck on a military base thousands of miles from home and family. Thanksgiving is such a homespun, simple holiday—none of the razzle-dazzle of Christmas or the explosive energy of the Fourth of July. Thanksgiving is a celebration of families, of gratitude and warmth and cozy reflections. And we had no one to reflect with, to share memories or gratitude.

On a walk a few days after my Thanksgiving complaint, I overheard a neighbor echoing my thoughts. I guess that's when the idea came to me and I dashed home, excited to put my plan into action.

I made a list of all the folks I knew who were in the same predicament as we; no nearby family, no familiar place to spend the holiday. And then I called each one, inviting them to bring something they would take if they were going to a Thanksgiving dinner at their parents' or grandparents'. Suddenly Thanksgiving was exciting again, and I looked forward to the day with anticipation.

There was no frost on the pumpkin, nor were there drying cornstalks or crispy leaves when the sun came up on that tropical Thanksgiving morning. But I still set the table with the warm harvest colors of bronze and gold. Great Grandma's ceramic turkey perched possessively at the center of the table, surrounded by pinecones I had gathered in the Pacific forest on my last trip home. I fixed the traditional tom turkey the way Mother used to do and stirred the cranberry relish again like Grandma had taught me years ago. A little world of memories emerged from the aroma of roasting turkey, tangy orange peel, and simmering cider and slowly filled the house like long-awaited friends.

My guests arrived with covered pots and chilled bowls of not only food but family recollections.

"My Aunt Sue Ellen's shrimp Jambalaya!" drawled one. "It just wouldn't be Thanksgiving without it!"

A young bachelor came bearing two pecan pies like golden trophies. "First pies I ever made!" he announced with a bit of awe at his own accomplishment. "I called my Gram down in Houston to get the recipe. Couldn't imagine Thanksgiving dinner without Gram's pies."

Others came with New England oyster dressing, Key Lime Pie, Iowa cornbread, Pacific Northwest salmon mousse, California fresh fruit salad, and even flaky *lumpia* from the Phillipines.

It was a crazy-quilt menu, one put together not by design but by delight—a meshing of different cultures, clans, and creativity. And when we joined our hands and bowed our heads to offer thanks, there was a joining of our hearts as well.

The conversations bubbled with sweet remembrances of Thanksgivings past, of family traditions, and regional customs. Each person shared a special insight and unique perspective on the holiday, and we fed ourselves not only on the banquet but also on the sense of fellowship.

It was a very special day. Each of us had discovered that Thanksgiving could be a day for making memories as well as recalling them. And now when I think of Thanksgiving, I am no longer limited by my childhood reminiscences of a gathering of aunts and uncles, cousins and grandparents. I have a new understanding of what it means to be a family, for I've learned we are a part of the family of Man. And whenever we sit together, sharing ourselves, our heritages, and our bits of home, our unity is magnified. And we find much for which to give thanks—much more than I had ever imagined!

Pamela Kennedy is a freelance writer of short stories, articles, essays, and children's books. Married to a naval officer and mother of three children, she has made her home on both U.S. coasts and currently resides in Hawaii. She draws her material from her own experiences and memories, adding bits of imagination to create a story or mood.

Housewife's Prayer

Phyllis C. Michael

Thank you, Lord,
   For kitchens where a kettle boils and sings;
Thank you, Lord,
   For cupboards filled with, oh, so many things;
Thank you, Lord,
   For pots and pans to cook the food we eat;
Thank you, Lord,
   For loved ones near to make the day complete.

Thank you, Lord,
   For cookies since the baking is such fun;
Thank you, Lord,
   For comfy chairs to rest in when work's done;
Thank you, Lord,
   For windows, where I watch the children play;
Thank you, Lord,
   For giving me the faith just now to pray.

Photo Opposite
THANKSGIVING KITCHEN
The Stock Market

Let's Be Thankful

Mary E. Reiter

The leaves are a riot of color along the edge of the road this fall. Red, yellow, rust, brown, and gold; beautiful scenery everywhere. It seems appropriate at the end of our lovely summer season that everything has flamed into unusual brilliance before fall leaves the trees stark and bare for the approaching winter.

By now most of the leaves have broken loose from their moorings and have rustled to earth. They have been dug out of the gutters, swept from the patios, and raked into piles. The lawn chairs and hammock have long since been stored away; the precious umbrella folded up and a protective covering put over it, the screens replaced with storm windows, the car winterized, and the furnace cleaned. The summer clothes have been packed away and the winter clothes hauled out. Even the last nasty job, hulling the walnuts, has been done.

But Indian Summer lasted so long that Thanksgiving time crept up on us before we realized it! This wonderful season of the year was here before we had time to plan for it or savor the joy and memories it brings.

My encyclopedia states that Thanksgiving Day in the United States is "a day set apart annually and appointed by the president for giving thanks to God for the favors and mercies of the year past."

"Come, ye thankful people, come!" we sing on Sunday morning at church—and suddenly we realize how many blessings we really have.

Life itself is truly a wondrous gift. What we do with it, of course, is up to each of us.

Being able to worship according to the dictates of one's own heart and conscience is a far greater luxury for which to be thankful than most people, at least in our own country, realize.

Here in the United States, most of us have the basics: food, shelter, and clothing. There are a good many people in the world today who would be more than satisfied if they could just enjoy the necessities that we take for granted.

Then there are family and friends to be grateful for. The Thanksgiving season is a good time to remember people, whether near at hand or far away. We really don't realize sometimes what a phone call, a card or note, or a visit, if possible, means to a loved one. So let's remember someone this Thanksgiving Day and actually do something to make their day brighter. And let's all be thankful for our faith, our country, and our families!

While looking through a book one day, I found this Thanksgiving poem that I would like to share with you:

A Good Thanksgiving

Annie Douglas Green Robinson

Said Old Gentleman Gay, "On a Thanksgiving Day,
If you want a good time, then give something away."
So he sent a fat turkey to Shoemaker Price,
And the shoemaker said, "What a big bird! How nice!
And, since such a good dinner's before me, I ought
To give poor Widow Lee the small chicken I bought."

"This fine chicken, oh, see!" said the pleased Widow Lee,
"And the kindness that sent it, how precious to me!
I would like to make someone as happy as I—
I'll give Washerwoman Biddy my big pumpkin pie."
"And, oh, sure!" Biddy said, " 'tis the queen of all pies!
Just to look at its yellow face gladdens my eyes!
Now it's *my* turn, I think; and a sweet ginger cake
For the motherless Finigan children I'll bake."

"A sweet cake all our own! 'Tis too good to be true!"
Said the Finigan children, Rose, Denny, and Hugh;
"It smells sweet of spice, and we'll carry a slice
To poor little lame Jake—who has nothing that's nice."
"Oh, I thank you and thank you!" said little lame Jake:
"Oh, what a bootiful, bootiful, bootiful cake!
And oh, such a big slice! I will save all the crumbs
And will give 'em to each little Sparrow that comes!"

And the Sparrows, they twittered, as if they would say,
Like Old Gentleman Gay, "On a Thanksgiving Day,
If you want a good time, then give something away!"

39

CRAFTWORKS

Mouse Doorstop

This adorable mouse tucked into bed for a nice snooze is actually a functional doorstop which can be made out of simple ingredients with glue and a little hand sewing. It will make a wonderful Christmas present.

Materials needed:
One brick
One piece of felt, any color, 13 by 13 inches
Craft glue
One piece of solid-color fabric, 13 by 13 inches, for bed
1⅝-inch gathered lace, approx. 27 inches, for bottom half of covered brick
One piece of print fabric, 7¼ by 7¼ inches, for coverlet
Two pieces of print fabric, 4¾ by 3 inches, for pillow
Polyester fiber-fill
⅞-inch gathered lace, approx. 17 inches, for pillow
One piece of solid-color fabric for a 4-inch circle (not to be hemmed) for bonnet
½-inch flat lace to go around bonnet
Gray felt, 5 by 8 inches, for mouse
Scrap of pink felt for mouse's ears and hands
Sequins for eyes
Small black bead for nose
Black thread for whiskers
Three 8-inch strands of gray yarn for mouse's tail

Step One: Covering Brick

Cover brick with felt as if wrapping a package and secure with glue. Cover felt-covered brick with solid-color fabric in same fashion and secure with glue.

Squeeze a line of glue on the top edge of the gathered 1⅝-inch lace and glue onto bottom half of brick to create dust ruffle.

Step Two: Sewing Coverlet, Pillow, and Bonnet

Turning under only once, stitch a ¼-inch hem around the 7¼-inch square of print fabric for bed coverlet. Set aside.

With wrong sides together, whipstitch pillow together on three sides and turn. Fill with polyester fiber-fill and close. Stitch the ⅞-inch lace along edges of pillow.

Cut a 4-inch circle from solid-color fabric for the bonnet and whipstitch ½-inch lace along the edge. Make two rows of running stitches ¼ inch from where the lace is joined to the fabric. Leave enough thread to pull into gather to fit mouse head.

Step Three: Constructing Mouse

Trace patterns and cut pieces out of gray and pink felt. With right sides together, whipstitch the front seam of pattern number 2. Lining up the nose of piece number 1 with the nose of number 2, whipstitch top of head to sides of head. Turn and stuff with polyester. Whipstitch body (number 3) to head along neck seam. Whipstitch back seam to

40

close and stuff with polyester, leaving about ½ inch of the fiber-fill sticking out of the bottom of the body.

Using the photograph as a model, glue the bonnet onto the mouse; glue on sequins for eyes; and stitch or glue a black bead on the tip of the mouse's nose. Create whiskers by drawing three long strands of black thread through the nose with a needle and trim.

Aligning the bases, tack the pink ears to the gray ears, fold at the centers, and whip together along the bottom. Glue the ears into place using the photograph as a guide.

Step Four: Assembling Doorstop

Place the finished mouse on the bed and secure the body with glue. Braid three strands of gray yarn for mouse tail. Secure with very narrow bow. Glue unfinished end of the tail onto the bed where it will not show after the cover is in place. Glue the ribbon end to the pillow.

Complete assembly by placing cover over the mouse's body, as shown, and spot-glue cover on the lower sides and along the end of the brick. Fold the hand pieces at the wrist and glue in place so that only the hands appear on top of the cover.

Clara Zuspann

Mrs. Clara Zuspann has been creating mouse ornaments as gifts for her family for years and believes that hobbies keep people of all ages healthy and happy. She makes her mouse doorstops in Evansville, Indiana.

CRAFTWORKS

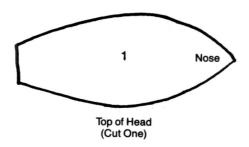

Top of Head
(Cut One)

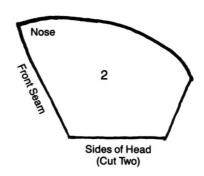

Sides of Head
(Cut Two)

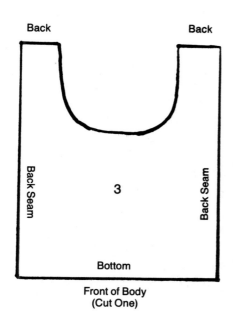

Front of Body
(Cut One)

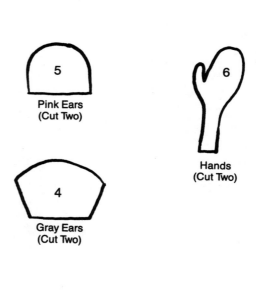

Pink Ears
(Cut Two)

Gray Ears
(Cut Two)

Hands
(Cut Two)

Pattern shown is actual size

Bread in the Baking

Gertrude Jesser

As the cool days of autumn come on the scene,
A strange nostalgia floats through my head.
I'm reminded of Mother's wood-burning range
And the luscious aroma of homemade bread.

No other smell could quite compare
With the fragrance of bread in the baking.
As mountain-like loaves emerged from the oven,
A "heel" was mine for the taking.

Today's magic ovens will do just as well;
So I'll gather ingredients together,
Give my family the treat of homemade bread
To enjoy whatever the weather.

Photo Opposite
THE STAFF OF LIFE
Dick Dietrich

A Slice of Life

Edgar A. Guest

Dear Lord, accept our humble prayer
Of thanks for all Thy watchful care;
For yield of field and vine and tree
Our hearts give gratitude to Thee;
Now lies the frost upon the vine,
We see another year decline;
But through the pain and strife and woe,
Thy blessings manifestly show.

Dear Lord, for laughter and for song
Which have been ours, for righted wrong,
For steps of progress we have made,
For all the works of art and trade,
For science which has conquered pain
And given hope where hope seemed vain;
For all that helps mankind to live,
This day to Thee our thanks we give.

Dear Lord, despite its pain and strife
We thank Thee for our richer life;
This is a better world for man
Than when this closing year began;
We who have suffered still can find
Proof of Thy love and mercy kind;
In all our works Thy hand we see
And bow in gratitude to Thee.

Edgar A. Guest began his illustrious career in 1895 at the age of fourteen when his work appeared in the Detroit Free Press. *His column was syndicated in over 300 newspapers, and he became known as "The Poet of the People." Mr. Guest captured the hearts of vast radio audiences with his weekly program, "It Can Be Done" and, until his death in 1959, published many treasured volumes of poetry.*

COME HOME

Douglas Malloch

Home's not a house, home is a heart
    To which you come at night;
Home is a shrine, a thing apart,
    An altar lamp alight.
The journey o'er, the long day through,
Home is a heart awaiting you.

How low your roof I do not care,
    How high your ivied towers;
If not a heart is waiting there
    That counts the weary hours,
You are as homeless as the poor
Who sleep unsheltered on the moor.

But if you have a hearth, a home,
    A chair, a glowing fire,
A wife awaiting while you roam,
    And children for their sire,
Let neither gold nor pleasure blind,
Nor think a greater joy to find.

Come home, for home is always best,
    However loud the song;
Come home, for home is tenderest,
    And right, and never wrong;
Come home, for fear some foolish day
You stay too long and lose the way.

Photo Opposite
THE WELCOMING HEARTH
Monserrate Schwartz

A Pageant at Thanksgiving

John Moring

The Pilgrims were first—
  first out of the classroom and first on stage.
Laughing, giggling, looking for a parent in the
  auditorium;
Maybe a little nervous.
Miles Standish said some words,
  though they weren't loud
  or even memorable.
But the words came from the heart of a seven-
  year-old:
A redhead with a Pilgrim hat over one eye
  and a cardboard musket held upside down.
The Indians came later,

looking fierce in brown paper-mâché.
They brought corn and plastic fish,
  and the Pilgrims invited them to the feast.
Orange and black and red and green.
Flashbulbs and smiles all about.
It was Plymouth as it should have been,
  full of excitement and thanksgiving.
Tiny Pilgrims, fierce Indians,
  giggling in costume,
  a resplendent paper turkey,
And a lesson in how it all began—
  and why.

A Thanksgiving Fable

Oliver Herford

It was a hungry pussycat upon Thanksgiving
   morn,
And she watched a thankful little mouse that
   ate an ear of corn.
"If I ate that thankful little mouse, how thankful he should be,
When he has made a meal himself, to make a
   meal for me!
Then with his thanks for having fed, and his
   thanks for feeding me,
With all *his* thankfulness inside, how thankful I
   shall be!"
Thus mused the hungry pussycat upon Thanksgiving Day;
But the little mouse had overheard and declined
   (with thanks) to stay.

Child's
Play

Grace

Thank you for
   The food we eat,
Thank you for
   The flowers so sweet,
Thank you for
   The birds that sing,
Thank you, God,
   For everything.

53

FROM MY
G·A·R·D·E·N
JOURNAL

Deana Deck

The Sweet Potato: A Minor Miracle

In this season of Thanksgiving, we tend to concentrate on expressing gratitude for the major miracles in life such as loved ones, health, happiness, peace, and prosperity. Minor miracles can be easily overlooked.

One such miracle is a plant which provides a traditional ingredient for the Thanksgiving feast yet is seldom singled out for recognition: the sweet potato vine. What other garden vegetable begins its life cycle as a lush green houseplant, brightening up the kitchen throughout the long dreary winter, then when transplanted into the garden in spring, provides a thick green ground cover in just about any soil—a ground cover that, when harvested in fall, provides bushels of delectable and nutricious edibles that can be stored whole or cooked and frozen for use all winter? If you doubt that the lowly sweet potato is the miraculous plant in question, let me put those doubts to rest.

For several years I have been recycling the offspring of a single sweet potato which I selected at random from a grocer's wire basket one snowy day in December. It has since become a personal challenge to see just how many years of houseplant/ground cover/edible harvest pleasure I can sustain from that one little vegetable.

To begin a never-ending cycle of your own this Thanksgiving, start by selecting a healthy, unblemished, medium-sized sweet potato. Next, you will need a container with an opening slightly larger in diameter than the sweet potato. I recall my grandmother using bright green prune juice bottles.

Insert three or four toothpicks into the potato at its "waistline" to provide a base of support. Position the potato so that the toothpicks rest on the container's mouth. Add water so that the bottom inch of the potato is immersed and maintain this water level over the next few weeks. The potato will begin to sprout roots and rust-colored and green shoots. As the plant matures, you will enjoy the vigorous red stems and handsome green and purple leaves which will fill your window.

I usually start two potatoes at the same time, because just as the plant matures into a really pretty addition to my kitchen window, it is time for the next step, which requires dismantling the plant entirely. Growing a second vine lets me have my cake and eat it too.

When your houseplant has stems that are four to five inches long, after roughly six to eight weeks of growing, it will be time to prepare slips for the garden. Remove the potato from the container and cut a chunk of potato for each stem. Plant these sections of stem and potato in small pots—I use styrofoam coffee cups with drainage holes punched in the bottom—and cover with fresh potting soil. Cultivate the plants in good light until all danger of frost is past. It is wise to harden off the plants by placing them outside on mild days a week before planting. Bring them back indoors if night temperatures drop into the forties. Do not transplant them into the garden until nights are consistently in the fifty-degree range. The best daytime growing temperature is sixty-five to ninety-five degrees, so depending on your local climate, your plants can be set out any time from mid-April on.

Choose a sunny location with fairly loose, well-drained soil. Heavy clay soils will need to be enhanced with peat or sand and compost. Plant your vines eighteen inches to two feet apart so they will have plenty of room to spread out. My own plants go in a bed

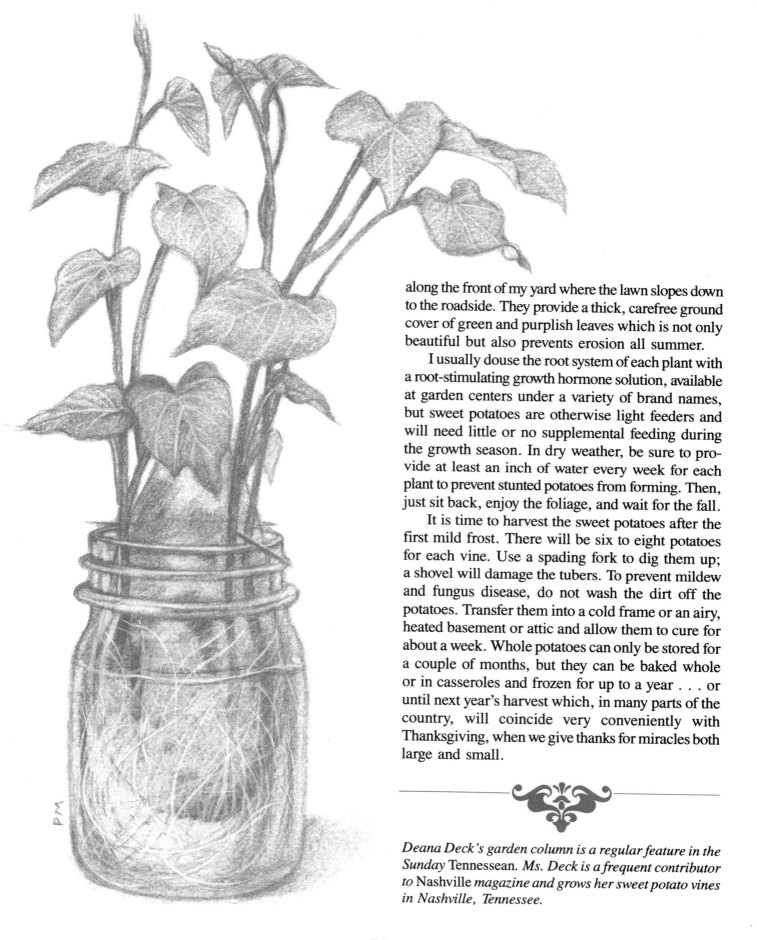

along the front of my yard where the lawn slopes down to the roadside. They provide a thick, carefree ground cover of green and purplish leaves which is not only beautiful but also prevents erosion all summer.

I usually douse the root system of each plant with a root-stimulating growth hormone solution, available at garden centers under a variety of brand names, but sweet potatoes are otherwise light feeders and will need little or no supplemental feeding during the growth season. In dry weather, be sure to provide at least an inch of water every week for each plant to prevent stunted potatoes from forming. Then, just sit back, enjoy the foliage, and wait for the fall.

It is time to harvest the sweet potatoes after the first mild frost. There will be six to eight potatoes for each vine. Use a spading fork to dig them up; a shovel will damage the tubers. To prevent mildew and fungus disease, do not wash the dirt off the potatoes. Transfer them into a cold frame or an airy, heated basement or attic and allow them to cure for about a week. Whole potatoes can only be stored for a couple of months, but they can be baked whole or in casseroles and frozen for up to a year . . . or until next year's harvest which, in many parts of the country, will coincide very conveniently with Thanksgiving, when we give thanks for miracles both large and small.

Deana Deck's garden column is a regular feature in the Sunday Tennessean. *Ms. Deck is a frequent contributor to* Nashville *magazine and grows her sweet potato vines in Nashville, Tennessee.*

The Approach of Thanksgiving

Eugene Field

There is a dawning in the sky
Which doth a world of fate imply,
And on each casual passing face,
A look expectant you may trace.
These signs the veteran turkey sees
And with a deep and mournful sigh,
He calls his numerous family nigh
And murmurs, pointing to the trees,
"Roost high, my little ones, roost high!"

Photo This Page
A TURKEY ON A SNOWY DAY
Grant Heilman

Pumpkins in the Cornfield

Adelaide Blanton

Pumpkins in the cornfield;
Fodder in the shock;
An ear of yellow-golden grain
Hangs on every stock.

Blackbirds flying here and there,
The yellow corn they spy;
But I'm not thinking of the corn;
I'm thinking pumpkin pie.

When Father Carves the Duck

Ernest Vincent Wright

We all look on with anxious eyes
When Father carves the duck;
And Mother almost always sighs
When Father carves the duck.
Then all of us prepare to rise
And hold our bibs before our eyes
And be prepared for some surprise
When Father carves the duck.

He braces up and grabs a fork
Whene'er he carves a duck,
And won't allow a soul to talk
Until he's carved the duck.
The fork is jabbed into the sides
Across the breast the knife he slides

While every careful person hides
From flying chips of duck.

The platter's always sure to slip
When Father carves a duck,
And how it makes the dishes skip!
Potatoes fly amuck!
The squash and cabbage leap in space,
We get some gravy in our face,
And Father mutters cryptic grace
Whene'er he carves a duck.

We then have learned to walk around
The dining room and pluck
From off the windowsills and walls
Our share of Father's duck,
While Father growls and blows and jaws
And swears the knife was full of flaws,
And Mother laughs at him because
He couldn't carve a duck.

That Old Two-Seated Hack

Ethel K. Gosney

Do you recall that old two-seated hack
Way back in the olden days?
When dressed in our best, we rode out in style
Behind two high-stepping bays.

Grandma and Mamma rode up front with Dad
With the little ones on their laps.
The rest of us snuggled down in the back seat,
All bundled up in our wraps.

Come Monday the back seat of that versatile hack
Was removed for the rest of the week
To make room for the dozens of jobs round the ranch,
For hauling or whatever the need.

Much hard work was done by that blessed old hack,
And often a trip into town,
But on Saturday the back seat was put back in place
And the hack cleaned and polished up and down.

Some folks had surreys with fringe on the top,
With mudguards and steps front and back.
But for everyday living most farm folks preferred
A down-to-earth two-seated hack!

Photo Opposite
THE OLD WAGON
GROTON, VERMONT
Dick Dietrich

Thanksgiving Trivia

When did the first Thanksgiving take place in America?

The actual first Thanksgiving in America is a matter of some dispute. The answer depends on whether you think of Thanksgiving as a harvest festival or as a commemoration of safe delivery from harm. French Huguenots in Florida dedicated June 30, 1564, as an official day of thanksgiving for God's goodness on their behalf. They were wiped out one year later by Spanish raiders, and with them went their designated day of celebration. In Maine a service of thanksgiving for safe travel was first held on August 7, 1607, by George Popham's colonists at the mouth of the Kennebec River. The Berkeley Hundred settlers established an official day of thanks to commemorate their safe arrival from England as early as November of 1619.

But it was the Plymouth Pilgrims in Massachusetts who first gave thanks for good crops, hence inaugurating Thanksgiving as an American harvest feast. New England Thanksgiving remained a regional event for over 100 years. Gradually other states adopted the practice.

Artist's rendering of Berkeley Hundred settlers giving thanks in November 1619
Courtesy of the Berkeley Plantation, Virginia

Noted historian Clifford Dowdey writes:

Some version of a thanksgiving celebration was as old as recorded history, going back to the Hebrews and the Greeks, and the Romans who copied it from them. In England, a thanksgiving was celebrated as a Harvest Home Day, and it was this custom that the Berkeley Hundred settlers followed on their safe arrival. Because New England had better propagandists, Thanksgiving has passed into legend as an invention of the Pilgrims. Actually, before the religious dissenters called Pilgrims ever set out from England . . . a thanksgiving celebration was introduced in the New World by that cross section of Britishers who founded a plantation in Tidewater Virginia.

PIECES

When was Thanksgiving first proclaimed an annual national holiday?

Despite singular proclamations for days of thanksgiving by George Washington, both Thomas Jefferson and John Quincy Adams considered such proclamations to be a violation of the division between church and state. It was not to be until Abraham Lincoln, hoping to bind together a nation torn by two years of civil war, proclaimed the last Thursday of November 1863 to be a day of national thanksgiving for the bountiful gifts of the land. The holiday was modeled after New England tradition, and northern armies were brought turkey and cranberries by grateful civilians. The second year of nationally celebrated Thanksgiving followed Sherman's September march through Georgia, and Lincoln urged his countrymen to give thanks to "The Great Disposer of Events" for restoring peace to the land once more.

To the poet, to the philosopher, to the saint, all things are friendly and sacred, all events profitable, all days holy, all men divine.

Ralph Waldo Emerson

Stand up, on this Thanksgiving Day, stand up upon your feet. Believe in man. Soberly and with clear eyes, believe in your own time and place. There is not and there never has been a better time or a better place to live in. Only with this belief can you believe in hope and believe in work.

Phillips Brooks

If the lesson out of all the sweet Thanksgiving periods of our lives only stirs in us some mighty impulse so to gladden other lives that the circle of grateful ones shall be increased, it will be doing for us and for others what God, doubtless, would best like it to do, and will make many a new strain of gratitude to swell the song to be sung one day when all the world shall praise Him.

Author Unknown

In this world, anyone who does not believe in miracles is not a realist.

Anonymous

The more we live by our intellect, the less we understand the meaning of life.

William James

NOVEMBER LANDSCAPE

Earle J. Grant

Mountain peaks are already
Tipped with snow;
And sweeping down the valley,
Chill winds blow,
Whipping sepia leaves
From off the trees,
Playing mournful cadence
Around the eaves.

Smoke rises from farmhouses
Like pungent incense,
Against the fall sunset's
Carmine and gold tints.
The cornshocks point
Brown fingers to the sky
While, overhead, wild geese
To the southland fly.

Pumpkins, potatoes, and apples
Fill the waiting bins.
Oh, let us count our blessings
Before the old year ends!

Photo Opposite
MOUNT SHUKSAN AT FIRST SNOW
WASHINGTON STATE
Walden Joura

The Latch upon the Gate

Douglas Malloch

The little hurts of childhood seem such little hurts to us—
Such foolish things to cry about, such silly things to fuss.
We often smile at children's tears, alas, we often frown—
I wish that from our eminence we elders could get down,
Get down and walk the children's world where little things are great,
Down where you have to climb to reach the latch upon the gate.

The little hurts of childhood seem little hurts to men;
That must be why we sear their souls with anger now and then.
When years have hardened us to ill, we oftentimes forget
That plastic as creation's clay are all the children yet.
If we would find the children's hearts and lead the children straight,
We must get down and climb to reach the latch upon the gate.

Grandma Moses

Cynthia Wyatt

There are several reasons why a person becomes a legend. They may possess bravery in the face of danger or vision in a time of darkness. They may sacrifice everything for a noble cause without complaint, or share their riches beyond expectation.

And then there are those who become known to

others because of their special gifts: athletes, dancers, singers, writers, and painters. When their gifts flourish despite a lack of nourishing education or economic advantage, they become legends indeed, people whose accomplishments exceed the possibilities of their surroundings. Grandma Moses is one of these legends.

Born Anna Mary Robertson, she grew up in simple rural surroundings in upstate New York. Her father was a farmer and an inventor, a man with an eye for beauty. He painted landscapes and once, while recuperating from an illness, painted a mural in their house. Anna's sister Sara entertained the younger children with her pencil drawings, and her sister Celestia actually took painting lessons as a teenager. The ability to make pictures was hardly anything special at all to the woman who would spend the last two decades of her 101 years of life as a world-famous artist.

When Anna married, her husband discouraged her from spending time on such "foolishness" as painting, but Anna made pictures to give as presents, and she decorated some of her furniture. When she was in her late sixties, her husband died. Too old for strenuous housework and cared for by her son and daughter-in-law, she found herself with the unthinkable—idle hands. As had her father before her, she reached for the materials with which to make pictures.

At first she worked in a sort of grospoint needlework style which she called "worsted pictures." Painful arthritis eventually led her to devote her time exclusively to oil paints. Her work was prolific, and soon there were so many pictures of farms and meadows and country people that she was persuaded to display them in a drugstore window in the little neighboring town of Hoosick Falls.

The rest is history. A traveling art collector happened to pass the store window, and two years later the world saw a one-woman show in New York City which introduced the octogenarian American genius, Grandma Moses.

Her pictures are enjoyable scenes of the countryside with flowing rivers and flowering trees, farm activities such as processing maple syrup or rounding up livestock, and family celebrations. Her style is primitive but shows an unquestionable eye for perspective, color, and the grouping of images. The world she depicts is full of people going about their business, none of whom attract special attention away from the whole.

Grandma Moses was a wise woman, and there is wisdom in her paintings, a serene sense of the proper order of things. Her method of painting also showed a rural wisdom. She believed that it was only correct to have a frame picked out before beginning a painting. "I always thought it a good idea to build the sty before getting the pig," she writes in her autobiography, *My Life's History*. "Likewise with young men, get the home before the wedding."

In many ways her world seems to have been closer to the mystery of life and death than most. "I never know how I'm going to paint until I start in; something tells me what to go right on and do." In the months before his unexpected death, her husband took sudden interest in her painting and told her that if he could come back and take care of her after death, he would. "It was as though he had something to do about this painting business," she writes.

There is a moving story about a dream her father had when she was a little girl. In the dream he saw his then tiny daughter in a large hall surrounded by applauding, cheering people, "And looking, I saw you, Anna Mary, coming my way, walking on the shoulders of men, . . . waving to me." Grandma Moses would still remember her father's dream ninety years later and wonder if it had foretold her future. "I often wonder, now that I am getting such kind, well-wishing letters from almost every country on the globe."

"Dreams," her father said, "cast their shadows before us."

Michael McKeever

Galapagos tortoise, one focus of the zoo's program

To Give Thanks, To Return What Was Taken

I knew I was being watched even as I turned my head. I was sitting on a large stone worn smooth by the tide. Here and there driftwood, bleached white by the sun and salt, lay scattered like whale bones along the California shoreline. It was morning; the sandstone bluffs behind me still cast their long shadows down the beach.

I looked down from my rock into the unblinking eyes of a harbor seal.

This happened on a stretch of the central coast north of Santa Barbara that is splendidly isolated. It was several miles to the nearest road and much farther to the nearest town. Consequently, the sea creatures there regard humans with more curiosity than dread.

The seal looked me over from ten feet away for nearly a minute, nose twitching slightly as it tried to pick up a familiar scent. There was a soft bark and the smell of fish in the air. Then, curiosity satisfied, it turned and waddled slowly back into the ocean.

For a moment I saw its head bobbing on the water near a floating island of kelp. Then it slipped beneath the surface and was gone.

"Good-bye, seal," I called into the wind. "Be careful of the fishing nets."

As I walked back down the beach, I reflected that while I had been of no help to it, at least I had brought it no harm.

The Chumash Indians who lived along the cen-

Przewalski's horses

sport," wrote an ancient Greek, "the frogs do not die in sport but in earnest."

Another writer, Fyodor Dostoevsky, scolded us in *The Brothers Karamazov*. "Love the animals," he wrote. "God has given them the rudiments of thought and joy untroubled. Don't trouble it, don't harass them, don't deprive them of their happiness, don't work against God's intent."

California condors

tral California Coast were a sea people. They hunted whales in great planked canoes, brawny oarsmen beating the waves with a steady rhythm. And when the whale was taken, the Chumash gave thanks, slicing off part of the whale's flesh and returning it to Mother Ocean.

The Chumash are almost completely gone now. Our ancestors ravaged them, scattering their rich culture to the wind like dried grass seeds.

We haven't done much better with the world they left behind. Sewage has been poured into the ocean's depths and oil smeared across its surface in an iridescent tide. The California grizzly the Chumash feared has been hunted down and exterminated. The California condor they worshipped is not far behind. There are even species of plants that have all but disappeared.

Some of the animals were killed for food, some because they were, in one way or another, a threat. Others, many others, were killed simply for the fun of it. "Though the boys throw stones at the frogs in

Happily there are people in the world who do not trouble the animals but instead, like the Chumash, try to return to the wild and free world a little of what was taken from it.

Balboa Park nestles in the heart of San Diego, California, like a precious stone. Surrounded by the bustling city's concrete and steel, the park's 1,400 acres are an oasis of grace and tranquility. In its century of existence, it has hosted two World's Fairs. Today its rolling lawns and lush gardens enhance a cornucopia of museums, theaters, and other pleasures.

But beyond a doubt, Balboa Park's crown jewel is the world-renowned San Diego Zoo. Its 128 acres teeming with life from every part of the world, the zoo is a top-ranking tourist attraction.

But the San Diego Zoo is far more than a Sunday

Central American green iguana

afternoon spent visiting the lions and tigers and bears. Its true heart and soul lies in a quiet yet desperate battle, a battle in which a single egg gives hope and a mewing baby animal is a victory. In the struggle to give back to the natural world that of which it was robbed, the San Diego Zoo is a leader.

Consider the Przewalski horse. Stocky, mule-like, bristly; it is not an animal of beauty and elegance. But in its gait are echoed the hoofbeats of a time before memory. Its ancestors prance across the painted rock walls of Lascaux. And the Paleolithic hunters who made those images in a French cave so long ago would recognize the Przewalski horse today.

But they would not find it in the wild. For two thousand years, Chinese chroniclers wrote

Przewalski's horses

of its roaming the vast deserts of western Asia. Genghis Khan's Mongols conquered an empire from its sturdy back. But the last wild individual was taken in 1947. And by the 1960s, even the rumors of sightings had stopped.

But the Przewalski horse survived in zoos across the world. The largest single herd today is in the San Diego Wild Animal Park. Sister to the zoo, the Wild Animal Park covers 1,800 acres of San Diego's dusty backcountry. There is plenty of room for small, fragile communities of animals to grow in strength and number.

And now plans are being made to return the Przewalski horse to Asia, to let it again run free and wild across the windswept Asian steppes.

There are precedents.

For millennia poets wrote and minstrels sang of the beautiful white oryx on the sands of Arabia. Its long twin horns, seen from a distance, seemingly merge, giving birth to the tale of the unicorn. But by the early 1970s, hunters in four-wheel-drive vehicles had gunned down the last free oryx.

But again zoos, including San Diego, came to the rescue. Carefully nourished herds of oryx in captivity increased in number. In 1978 the first shipment of oryx returned to the Hashemite Kingdom of Jordan where they flourished under the protection of the government.

Four years later the sultanate of Oman received its first shipment to be reintroduced. Today the Harasis tribesmen of the Jiddat Desert watch over the growing herds of white oryx.

For the California condor, however, survival still hangs in a precarious balance.

Bali mynah, another endangered species

Bali mynah or Rothschild's grackle

Miwok Indians danced in its honor. The Miwok heard thunder in its nine-and-a-half-foot wings and believed that the great bird brought rain.

But progress brought only death to the California condor. Where once thousands beat the air with their huge wings, only twenty-eight survive in the Los Angeles and San Diego zoos. The last free wild California condor was captured on April 9, 1987.

But in the sanctuaries of the zoos, there is hope. Two California condors, hatched in captivity, are now courting at the Wild Animal Park. There will be more eggs.

Perhaps one day the magnificent birds will soar again in the California sky. And the spirits of the Miwok will dance in thankful joy.

___

Michael McKeever is a Contributing Editor of Country Inns *magazine and a frequent contributor to* Physicians Travel. *At journey's end, Michael enjoys returning home to Imperial Beach, California.*

Like the Przewalski horse and white oryx, the California condor is an ancient animal. The

Arabian oryx

Photo Overleaf
WINTER'S FIRST LIGHT SNOW
NEW HAMPSHIRE
Dick Smith

November
Song

Evelynn Merilatt Boal

One leaf hangs on our little redbud tree.
One golden, heart-shaped harbinger of hope—
The autumn winds have failed to shake it free.
It lingers in the fall kaleidoscope.
These frigid mornings, every blade of grass
Is white with frost—November's well along.
The other leaves have blown away *en masse*.
But this one clings for its November song.
Alone, it waits to see the season end.
The cold collects in the November sky.
Those icy hints of wintertime impend
As graying days plod mercilessly by.
One morning, when I look, it will have flown
To keep the tryst it struggled to postpone.

Let Winter Come

Sudie Stuart Hager

Let winter come. The year has brought
A springtime rare and long,
A rainbow-tinted world brimful
Of laughter, bloom, and song;
A June of radiant loveliness—
A wedding in her train—
Fruit that ripened rich and full
In summer sun and rain;
Golden autumn days with clouds
Too thin to mar the blue;
Oh, He who made these seasons bright
Will bless the winter too!

79

Readers' Forum

You have given me great pleasure over the years with Ideals.

Geraldine Whites
Saint John, New Brunswick
Canada

On January 7, 1989, a special reader of yours passed away. His name was David Hallett. He was seventy-eight years old. He was a wonderful person, a best friend, and most of all a very special Grandpa. He was a very faithful reader of your magazine and read his favorite poems to my sister, Mary, and me frequently. Not only have your magazines touched his heart but also the hearts of our whole family. I'd like to express my thanks for making his reading time so special.

Mrs. Barbara Sloat
Sayres, Pennsylvania

I enjoy your beautiful books very much and treasure each and every issue.

Eunice Shellenberger
Palmer Lake, Colorado

Being a homeschool family, we are always looking for new learning tools. We wanted to let you know that our children are learning about poetry and more from your wonderful publication. Each new issue is a special treat, and we also used part of your Christmas and Easter issues for family devotions. Thank you ever so much for being a positive influence in our lives.

The Drew Hamann Family
Toledo, Ohio

Your magazine brings much joy and inspiration to me and to my elderly friend, an Alzheimers victim. She looks long and lovingly at the pictures.

Sister Grace Diethorn
Pittsburgh, Pennsylvania

It was a snowy, cold, blustery day here in Whiting, New Jersey, and I stepped ''gingerly'' and very slowly on the slippery walk to my mailbox which is some distance from my house. There in the mailbox was my copy of Ideals. What a lift to my spirit! A joy! A delight! When I returned to the house and slipped the magazine out of its wrapper to glance through quickly, I found it difficult to put down—such very beautiful photography and poetry! . . .

   May the Lord richly bless all of you who are involved in the publication of this very fine magazine.

Ms. Dorothy Ahlers
Whiting, New Jersey

I have always enjoyed the beautiful poetry and photos in Ideals.

Lanita Stallings
Madison, Tennessee

I have been reading Ideals for the past year and it is a beautiful publication. There are very few publications now that show the spirit of gentleness and the genuine quality of this magazine.

Ann Marie Eller
Mechanicsville, Virginia

Want to share your crafts and recipes?
Readers are invited to submit original craft ideas and original recipes for possible development and publication in future *Ideals* issues. Please send recipes or query letters for craft ideas (with photograph, if possible) to Editorial Features Department, Ideals Publishing Corporation, P.O. Box 140300, Nashville, Tennessee 37214-0300. Please do not send craft samples; they cannot be returned.

Celebrating Life's Most Treasured Moments

Artwork Opposite
THANKSGIVING HARVEST
Francis Chase